Crave-Worthy Candy Confections

WITH A SIDE OF SCIENCE

An Augmented Recipe Science Experience

by M. M. Eboch

CAPSTONE PRESS
a capstone imprint

Download the Capstone app!

- Ask an adult to download the Capstone 4D app.
- Scan the cover and stars inside the book for additional content.

When you scan a spread, you'll find fun extra stuff to go with this book! You can also find these things on the web at www.capstone4D.com using the password: candy.10713

Snap Books are published by Capstone Press,1710 Roe Crest Drive, North Mankato, Minnesota 56003
www.mycapstone.com

Library of Congress Cataloging-in-Publication Data
Names: Eboch, M. M., author.
Title: Crave-worthy candy confections with a side of science / by M.M. Eboch.
Description: North Mankato, Minnesota : Capstone Press, [2019] | Series: Snap books. Sweet eats with a side of science 4D | Series: 4D, an augmented recipe science experience | Audience: Age 9-14.
Identifiers: LCCN 2018011648 (print) | LCCN 2018019012 (ebook) |
  ISBN 9781543510751 (eBook PDF) |
  ISBN 9781543510713 (library binding)
Subjects: LCSH: Desserts—Juvenile literature. | Candy—Juvenile literature.
  | LCGFT: Cookbooks.
Classification: LCC TX773 (ebook) | LCC TX773 .E325 2019 (print) | DDC
  641.86—dc23
LC record available at https://lccn.loc.gov/2018011648

Editorial Credits
Abby Colich, editor; Juliette Peters, designer;
Tracy Cummins, media researcher; Laura Manthe, production specialist

Photo Credits
Photo and Food Stylist: Sarah Schuette; All images by Capstone Studio/Karon Dubke; except: Shutterstock: Ahanov Michael, 30 Top Right, 30 Middle Left, ffolas, 30 Top Left, Geshas, 30 Bottom Right, Imageman, 30 Bottom Left, iva, 13, Mr. Meijer, 30 Middle Right

Printed in the United States of America.
PA017

Table of Contents

Make Candy in your Kitchen

Imagine having your very own science lab. It has plenty of space. It has all of the materials you need for your experiments. It has tools to measure those materials. It even has a source of heat. Basically, it's a kitchen!

Making candy is like doing science experiments. Ingredients are mixed together and heated. Reactions occur. You don't need to know how the science works. However, it can be helpful to know why taffy is chewy and lollipops are hard. Understanding what happens, and why, can help you if something goes wrong.

KITCHEN SAFETY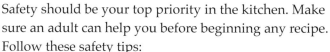

Safety should be your top priority in the kitchen. Make sure an adult can help you before beginning any recipe. Follow these safety tips:

- Wash your hands before beginning any recipe. Wash them again after touching raw ingredients such as eggs.

- Use caution when cooking at high temperatures. Be careful when touching hot pots, utensils, or food. Use a pot holder or oven mitt when transfering hot items.

- Take care when adding ingredients. Candy mixtures may bubble and splatter. Don't let the hot mixture touch your skin. It can cause burns.

- Use caution when using a sharp knife.

NOW HEAD TO YOUR KITCHEN SCIENCE LAB FOR SOME TASTY EXPERIMENTS!

HOTTER MEANS HARDER

To make most candy, you boil a mixture that includes sugar and water. As this syrup cooks, water boils away. The sugar becomes more concentrated. The mixture is cooked until it reaches a certain temperature. That high point determines how hard or soft your candy will be.

A candy thermometer helps you cook your mixture the right amount. If the temperature is too high or too low, the candy may turn out too hard or too soft. A mistake of only a few degrees can ruin a batch of candy. Always watch the pot and your thermometer closely. Otherwise you might not see when the temperature hits its target.

CONVERSION CHART

The recipes in this book use U.S. measurements. If you need metric measurements, here's a handy conversion guide.

VOLUME

1/4 teaspoon = 1.2 mL
1/2 teaspoon = 2.5 mL
1 teaspoon = 5 mL
1 tablespoon = 15 mL
1/4 cup = 60 mL
1/3 cup = 80 mL
1/2 cup = 120 mL
2/3 cup = 160 mL
3/4 cup = 180 mL
1 cup = 240 mL

TEMPERATURE

235°F = 113°C
240°F = 115°C
242°F = 116°C
245°F = 118°C
250°F = 121°C
260°F = 127°C
300°F = 149°C

TIP......................................

Always wash candy thermometers by hand. Dishwashers can cause them to lose accuracy.

Cinnamon Heart Lollipops

Show some love with heart-shaped lollipops! These pretty, tasty treats are great for holidays or anytime. Use another shape if you don't have heart molds. You'll cook this candy at a high temperature so it turns out hard.

INGREDIENTS

2 cups sugar
1/2 teaspoon cream of tartar
1/2 cup light corn syrup
1/2 cup cherry juice
dash of ground cinnamon
colored sanding sugar or
    sparkling sugar

SUPPLIES

heart-shaped lollipop molds
nonstick cooking spray
paper towel
lollipop sticks
measuring cups and spoons
medium saucepan
metal (heatproof) spoon
candy thermometer
plastic wrap

1 Spray the lollipop molds lightly with nonstick cooking spray. Gently wipe out the molds with a paper towel, leaving only a very thin layer of the spray. Place the lollipop sticks in the molds.

2 In a medium saucepan, combine the sugar, cream of tartar, corn syrup, and cherry juice over medium-high heat. Stir well. Bring to a boil. Stir regularly to dissolve the sugar.

3 Attach the candy thermometer to the saucepan. Without stirring, cook until the temperature reaches 300°F (adjust for altitude if necessary), about 20 minutes.

4 Remove the mixture from the heat. Stir in the cinnamon. Allow the bubbles to break up and disappear.

5 Use a metal spoon to carefully scoop up a heaping spoonful of the mixture. Gently spoon the mixture into a lollipop mold. Make sure the end of the lollipop stick is entirely covered.

6 Quickly repeat step 5 until all the mixture has been used. If the syrup becomes too thick, warm it over low heat.

7 Sprinkle colored or sparkling sugar over the lollipops. Allow the lollipops to cool.

8 Remove the the lollipops from the molds. Wrap individually in plastic wrap. Store them in an airtight container at room temperature.

TIP.............................

To measure corn syrup, first spray the measuring cup with nonstick spray. The corn syrup will pour out more easily.

Kitchen Science

HEAT IS ENERGY

Everything is made up of molecules. Molecules are tiny particles that are too small to see. They are constantly vibrating, although we can't see or feel this. Heat is a form of energy that moves between molecules. Put a pot of water on the stove and turn on the heat. The heat from the stove transfers to the molecules in the pot. Then it transfers to the molecules in the water. As the water heats, its molecules vibrate faster. Molecules can combine in different ways too. For example, sugar and water molecules bind together. Some of the water evaporates, turning into steam. All this is caused by the addition of heat. In scientific terms, cooking is just transferring energy by adding heat.

Gummy Stars

Gummy candies are fun to make and to eat! These colorful stars are great to snack on or to share with friends. The orange gummies are tart while the grape gummies are sweet. Once you've mastered this recipe, you can experiment with different flavors of juice and colors.

INGREDIENTS

1/2 cup unflavored gelatin, separated
1/4 cup cold water
2/3 cup grape juice
2/3 cup no-pulp orange juice
1/2 cup corn syrup or honey, separated
purple and orange food coloring

SUPPLIES

measuring cups
medium saucepan
star-shaped molds
metal spoon

1 Place 1/4 cup gelatin in 1/4 cup cold water. Allow to soften for about 5 minutes.

2 In a medium saucepan, combine the softened gelatin with the grape juice and 1/4 cup corn syrup or honey. Cook over medium heat until the gelatin dissolves.

3 Add several drops of purple food coloring. Carefully spoon the hot mixture into the molds. The gummy candy shrinks as it cools, so fill the molds as full as possible.

TIP......................

If a recipe says that an ingredient is separated, that means the total amount listed will not be used at once. Read through the recipe to see how much is needed at one time.

4 Refrigerate the candy for 1 hour, until firm. Unmold and store in an airtight container.

5 Repeat steps 1 through 4 using the orange juice and orange food coloring for the orange gummy candy.

Kitchen Science

HEAT AND TEMPERATURE ★

Temperature is a way of measuring energy. However, two things can have different amounts of energy at the same temperature. It depends on the number of molecules. Water has more molecules than air. A pot of water contains more molecules than the same pot full of air. With more molecules, the pot of water has more energy than the pot of air. This means water heated to 250°F (121°C) feels hotter than air heated to 250°F (121°C). You can quickly place a pan into an oven heated to 250°F (121°C) without being hurt. If you stick your hand into water heated to 250°F (121°C), you would get a severe burn! (Don't try this!) The water has more energy, which would transfer into your hand. That energy, in the form of heat, causes a burn.

Bacon Nut Brittle

What's better than crunchy, salty nut brittle? How about nut brittle with bacon! The combination of flavors—a touch of sweet and a touch of savory—makes for an unusual but tasty treat.

INGREDIENTS

8 slices of thick cut, smoked
　bacon
1/2 cup water
2 cups sugar
1 stick unsalted butter
1/3 cup light corn syrup
1/2 teaspoon baking soda
2 cups roasted, salted cashews
1 teaspoon vanilla extract
coarse salt for sprinkling

SUPPLIES

cutting board
knife
nonstick cooking spray
baking sheet
parchment paper
large heatproof spoon
large saucepan
measuring cups and spoons
candy thermometer

1 Cook the bacon according to package instructions until crispy. Cool on paper towels. On a cutting board, chop the bacon into 0.25- to 0.5-inch (1- to 2-cm) pieces.

2 Line the baking sheet with parchment paper and spray with nonstick cooking spray. Spray the large spoon as well.

3 In the large saucepan, combine the water, sugar, butter, and corn syrup. Bring to a boil, stirring occasionally.

4 Attach a candy thermometer to the saucepan. Continue cooking the mixture over medium to high heat, stirring occasionally. Cook until the candy thermometer reaches 300°F (adjusted for altitude if necessary), about 10 to 15 minutes. The caramel should be light brown, the color of a paper bag.

5 Remove the saucepan from the heat. Carefully stir in the baking soda, which will cause the mixture to bubble.

6 Stir in the cashews, vanilla extract, and bacon.

7 Immediately pour the brittle onto the baking sheet. Using the back of the large spoon, spread the brittle into a thin, even layer.

8 Lightly sprinkle the salt over the brittle. Let cool completely, about 30 minutes.

9 Break the brittle into large shards. Store in an airtight container at room temperature for up to one month.

Kitchen Science

HIGH-LEVEL COOKING ★

At sea level, water boils at 212 degrees Fahrenheit (°F), or 100 degrees Celsius (°C). At higher altitudes, there are fewer molecules in the air. The air is lighter, so it doesn't push down as heavily on things. This affects how water boils. If you live above sea level, you can figure out your boiling point with some simple math. For every 1,000 feet (305 m) you are above sea level, subtract two degrees Fahrenheit from the recipe temperature. If you live 2,000 feet (610 m) above sea level, for example, water will boil at 208°F (98°C). You would take four degrees off the temperature called for in each recipe.

Vanilla Nougat

Want to pretend you are in ancient Rome? Make some nougat! Historians believe Romans made nougat in the AD 100s. Today nougat can be found all over the world. This recipe is for an Italian-style nougat. It's cooked at a low temperature, making it chewy but soft and light.

INGREDIENTS

3 egg whites, at room temperature
1 cup sugar
1/2 cup corn syrup
1/4 cup water
1 tablespoon vanilla extract
1/2 teaspoon salt
2 cups shelled pistachios
1 cup dried cranberries
additional pistachios and cranberries to decorate

SUPPLIES

8- x 8-inch (20- x 20-cm) pan
parchment paper
nonstick cooking spray
electric mixer with whisk attachment
measuring cups and spoons
medium mixing bowl
medium saucepan
candy thermometer
rubber spatula

1 Line the pan with parchment paper. Spray the paper with nonstick cooking spray.

2 Add whisk attachment to electric mixer. Put the egg whites in the medium bowl. Set aside.

3 Combine the sugar, corn syrup, and water in a medium saucepan. Attach the candy thermometer to the saucepan. Bring to a boil over medium heat. Continue to boil without stirring until the mixture reaches 235°F (adjusted for altitude if necessary), about 6 minutes.

4 While the mixture continues to cook, start whipping the egg whites on low speed. Whip until they become a little frothy, about 1 minute.

5 Continue cooking the sugar syrup until it reaches 260°F. Slowly add the hot sugar syrup to the egg whites, mixing constantly. Try to avoid letting the syrup hit the rim of the bowl or the whisk attachment.

6 Increase the mixer speed to medium. Continue whipping until the nougat reaches a full, frothy foam, about 2 to 5 minutes.

7 Add the vanilla extract and salt to the nougat. Keep whipping until it forms stiff peaks, about 3 to 5 more minutes.

8 Remove the bowl from the mixer. Use a rubber spatula to mix in the pistachios and cranberries.

9 With rubber spatula spread the nougat in the pan in an even layer. Decorate the nougat by pressing additional pistachios and cranberries into the top in a pattern. Let set at room temperature for at least 2 hours, up to overnight.

10 Cut nougat into small squares. Store in an airtight container at room temperature for up to three days. You can also store nougat in the freezer for up to two months. Thaw for an hour in the refrigerator before eating.

TIP......................................

To separate an egg yolk from the white, crack the egg over a bowl. Let the whites fall into the bowl while moving the yolk between the two halves of the open shell. Continue this motion until all the egg white has fallen into the bowl. Save the yolk for another use or discard.

Rock Candy

Who wants to eat rocks? Everyone will when you make rock candy! Rock candy is simply sugar and water. The mixture is heated to concentrate the sugar. Then it is cooled slowly, which allows the sugar to reform into large crystals. As the water evaporates, sugar crystals form on the stick. It takes a week or so for big sugar crystals to form. Make sure you have a place to leave your jars undisturbed for that time.

INGREDIENTS

2 cups water
6 cups sugar
1/4 teaspoon lemon extract
1/4 teaspoon lime extract
yellow and green food coloring
sugar
powdered sugar or nonstick
    cooking spray

SUPPLIES

2 clean glass jars, each about
    1 quart
measuring cups and spoons
medium saucepan
wooden spoon
ladle
2 bamboo skewers or popsicle
    sticks
2 clean cloths or dish towels

1 Clean and dry the jars. Set aside.

2 Heat the water in the saucepan over medium-high heat. Bring it to a boil.

3 Pour the sugar into the water, stirring constantly with the wooden spoon. Continue to stir until the sugar dissolves and the mixture turns clear. Keep stirring just until the mixture boils rapidly.

4 As soon as the mixture boils, remove the saucepan from the heat. Let cool for 20 minutes.

5 Carefully ladle the sugar syrup into each jar, dividing equally. Add lemon extract and several drops of yellow food coloring to one jar. Add lime extract and several drops of green food coloring to the other jar. Stir to mix.

6 Place the jars in the refrigerator for about 1 hour.

7 Dip the bamboo skewers or popsicle sticks in water. Roll the bottom half of each in sugar. Remove the jars from the refrigerator and place one skewer into each. Be sure the tops of the skewers stick out above the liquid in the jars.

8 Drape a cloth over the jars to keep out dust. Leave the jars where they won't be disturbed for up to two weeks. Check each day to see how the crystals are forming, but don't move the jars.

9 In a week or so, remove the crystal-coated sticks and let them dry. Discard any leftover liquid. Store the rock candy in a sealed container. To keep them from getting sticky, dust the candy with powdered sugar or spray it with nonstick cooking spray.

Kitchen Science

SUGAR CRYSTALS

When you make rock candy, sugar dissolves in water. Hot water can hold more dissolved sugar than cold water can. You heat the water so more sugar can dissolve. The water becomes saturated with sugar. That means the water holds all the sugar it possibly can. As the syrup slowly cools down, it can no longer hold as much sugar. It becomes supersaturated. It contains more sugar than the solution can hold. The sugar comes out of the solution, forming crystals. When you wet your skewer and roll it in sugar, you are "seeding" your rock candy. The crystals grow on the "seeds" of sugar, creating larger crystals. The syrup needs to cool a little before you add the seeds. Otherwise the seeds would simply dissolve in the hot syrup. The cooler syrup won't dissolve the "seed" sugar.

Tiger Fudge

Serve this tiger fudge at a party and you're sure to get a roar of approval! This chocolate fudge is topped with peanut butter for double the yummy! Then it's drizzled with even more chocolate to look like the stripes of a tiger.

INGREDIENTS

2/3 cup evaporated milk
2 cups sugar
2 tablespoons unsalted butter
1/2 teaspoon salt
2 cups miniature marshmallows
1 cup semisweet or dark
    chocolate chips
1 teaspoon vanilla extract
1/2 cup peanut butter
1/4 cup chopped chocolate bar
    or melting chocolate

SUPPLIES

8- x 8-inch (20- x 20-cm) pan
aluminum foil
nonstick cooking spray
large saucepan
measuring cups and spoons
large wooden spoon
metal spoon
microwave-safe bowl

1 Line the bottom and sides of the pan with foil, leaving some foil overhanging the edges. Spray the foil with nonstick cooking spray.

2 In the saucepan combine the evaporated milk, sugar, butter, and salt. Place over medium-high heat.

3 Stirring constantly, bring the mixture to a rapid boil. Continue to stir constantly and boil for 5 more minutes.

4 Remove the saucepan from the heat. Add the marshmallows, chocolate chips, and vanilla extract. Stir until everything is combined and smooth.

5 Pour mixture into the pan and spread it evenly.

6 Heat the peanut butter in the microwave for 30 seconds. Slowly pour over the fudge. Spread over the fudge with the back of a spoon.

7 Melt the chopped chocolate in a microwave-safe bowl for 30 seconds. Stir and microwave again in 10-second increments until fully melted. Use a spoon to drizzle chocolate over the fudge.

8 Let cool until the fudge is firm, about 45 minutes. Use the foil to lift the fudge out of the pan. Peel off the foil and cut the fudge into squares. Store in an airtight container.

Chocolate Raspberry Truffles

Ooh la la! Truffles look fancy and taste delicious. Truffles are bite-sized candies formed into a ball. They can be as simple as chocolate and cream heated together. However, many truffles have other flavors and decorative coatings. Candy shops may sell them at a high price, but they're fairly easy to make at home. Truffles have to cool twice, so allow several hours to make.

INGREDIENTS	SUPPLIES
1 cup fresh raspberries	baking sheet
1/4 cup heavy cream	wax paper
1 cup semisweet chocolate chips	paper towels
1 teaspoon raspberry extract	medium saucepan
1 cup chocolate candy coating	measuring cups and spoons
	heatproof rubber spatula
	forks
	microwave-safe bowl

1 Line the baking sheet with waxed paper. Rinse the raspberries and pat them dry with paper towels.

2 Place the cream in the saucepan over medium heat. Bring just to a simmer.

3 Remove the cream from the heat. Add the chocolate chips and stir gently with the spatula until smooth. Stir in the raspberry extract.

4 Drop six to eight raspberries into the chocolate mixture. Try to gently coat each raspberry with chocolate, without breaking up the raspberry.

5 Use two forks to remove each chocolate-covered raspberry. Let the excess chocolate mixture drip back into the saucepan. Then place the chocolate-covered raspberry on the baking sheet.

6 Add additional raspberries to the chocolate, working in small batches.

7 Chill the truffles in the refrigerator until firm, at least 1 hour.

8 Melt the chocolate candy coating according to package directions. Allow the coating to cool until it is barely warm but not getting too stiff. Using a spoon or fork, dip a truffle into the coating. Allow excess coating to drip back into the bowl. Set the truffle back on the baking sheet. Repeat for all the truffles. If the candy coating gets too stiff, warm it gently in the microwave.

9 Return the baking sheet to the refrigerator. Chill the truffles for about half an hour.

10 Store truffles in the refrigerator. Leave space between them so they don't stick together.

Kitchen Science

EMULSIONS

Truffles start with a mix of chocolate and cream, called ganache. Ganache is an emulsion. An emulsion is a mixture of two liquids that will not combine together. The molecules in water cannot bind with the molecules in oil. Sometimes the ganache emulsion breaks, leaving a thin layer of oil on top of the chocolate. If this happens and the ganache is still warm, try whisking it. After a minute or two, it may blend properly. If the ganache has cooled, gently warm it while stirring often.

Apple Cider Caramels

As sugar heats, it begins to change flavor, and what a wonderful flavor it is! This chemical reaction is called caramelization. Sugar turns brown when heated. This gives caramels their color. Our chewy caramels start with apple cider. The cider flavor lingers on the tongue after the caramel flavor fades. Add coconut on top for a unique treat.

INGREDIENTS

2 cups apple cider
1/2 teaspoon ground cinnamon
1/4 teaspoon ground ginger
1/4 teaspoon ground nutmeg
2 cups sugar
1 1/2 cups heavy cream
1 cup corn syrup
4 tablespoons unsalted butter,
    plus more for cutting
1/2 teaspoon salt
shredded toasted coconut

SUPPLIES

8- x 8-inch (20- x 20-cm) baking
    pan
parchment paper
nonstick cooking spray
heavy-bottom, deep saucepan
measuring cups and spoons
mixng spoon
candy thermometer
cutting board
knife

1 Line the baking pan with parchment paper. Let some paper overhang on two opposite sides. Spray the parchment paper with nonstick cooking spray.

2 In the saucepan, combine the apple cider, cinnamon, ginger, and nutmeg. Bring to a low boil over medium heat. Simmer until the liquid has reduced to about 1/2 cup, about 20 minutes.

3 Add the sugar, cream, corn syrup, and butter to the saucepan. Stir to dissolve the sugar as you bring the mixture to a boil over high heat.

4 Reduce the temperature to medium-high. Attach the candy thermometer to the saucepan. Cook without stirring until the temperature reaches 250°F (adjusted for altitude if necessary), about 30 minutes.

5 As soon as the temperature reaches 250°F, remove the saucepan from the heat. Stir in the salt.

6 Pour the mixture into the baking pan. Evenly sprinkle shredded coconut on top. Let the dish stand for 12 to 18 hours at room temperature.

7 Use the parchment paper to lift the caramel out of the pan. Turn it out onto a cutting board. Cut the caramels into 1-inch (2.5-cm) squares. For ease of cutting, have an adult help you butter a sharp knife and use a gentle sawing motion. When the caramel begins sticking to the knife, add more butter.

TIP

The maximum temperature of the mixture determines how soft the caramels are. If you want softer caramels, boil the mixture only to 242 to 245°F. These soft caramels will need to be refrigerated for about 15 minutes before cutting.

Kitchen Science

STICK TO IT ★

Many candies, such as caramels, are sticky when you make them. Candy can also get stickier over time. That's because the sugar in the candy can absorb water from the air. The more moisture the air has, the stickier the candy can become. As the candy absorbs this extra water, it becomes stickier. Corn syrup molecules can absorb even more water than sugar molecules. Candy made with corn syrup can get even stickier than candy made only with sugar. Always store candy in an airtight container. This helps keep moist air away from the candy.

Double Chocolate Turtles

Take a look at these chocolate-coated clusters of nuts. Do they remind you of a certain animal? Turtles include any type of nut, caramel, and chocolate. This recipe uses two kinds of chocolate and also adds pretzels. The pretzels make for a great mix of salty and sweet.

INGREDIENTS

3 cups miniature pretzels
3 cups whole roasted pecans
1 stick unsalted butter
1 cup brown sugar
1/2 cup corn syrup
dash of salt
1/2 cup + 2 tbsp sweetened
    condensed milk (half of
    a 14-ounce can)
1/2 teaspoon vanilla extract
3/4 cup milk chocolate chips

3/4 cup semisweet or
    dark chocolate chips
1/2 teaspoon vegetable oil, separated

SUPPLIES

baking sheets
parchment paper
large saucepan
measuring cups and measuring spoons
candy thermometer
medium microwave-safe bowl

1 Line the baking sheets with parchment paper. Place the pretzels flat on the baking sheets. Leave at least 2 inches (5 cm) between each pretzel. Place two or three pecans on each pretzel.

2 In a large saucepan, combine the butter, brown sugar, corn syrup, and salt. Bring to a boil over medium heat. Add the sweetened condensed milk and vanilla extract.

3 Attach a candy thermometer to the saucepan. Cook until the temperature reaches 235 to 240°F (adjusted for altitude if necessary).

4 Working quickly, drop spoonfuls of caramel over the pecan clusters. Make sure some caramel touches each of the pecans and the pretzels. Cool until the caramel turns firm.

5 Place the milk chocolate chips and 1/4 teaspoon oil in a bowl. Melt in the microwave at 50 percent power, stirring every 30 seconds, until the chips are fully melted. Drop spoonfuls of chocolate on half of the turtles. Repeat this step with the semisweet or dark chocolate chips and remaining 1/4 teaspoon of oil. Use this chocolate to top the remaining half of the turtles.

6 Cool for 1 to 2 hours, or 30 minutes in the refrigerator. Store in an airtight container.

TIP. . . . .

This recipe includes caramel, but it's softer than in the apple cider caramel recipe. It stays softer because the caramel is not heated to such a high temperature. The softer caramel can more easily spread over the pecans and pretzels.

After-Dinner Mints

The after-dinner mint is a classic way to freshen your breath after a meal. The burst of mint leaves your mouth feeling fresh. In this recipe you'll create three different flavors, making these a great treat anytime.

INGREDIENTS

4 tablespoons salted butter, softened
2 cups confectioners' sugar, plus extra for dusting
1 tablespoon cream or milk
red and green liquid food coloring
1/2 teaspoon strawberry extract
1/4 teaspoon mint extract
1/2 teaspoon vanilla extract

SUPPLIES

large bowl
electric mixer
measuring cups and spoons
3 small bowls
cutting board
plastic wrap
two baking sheets
parchment paper
knife

1 In a large bowl use the electric mixer to beat the butter until creamy. With mixer on low, beat in sugar and cream or milk. Combine well.

2 Evenly divide the mixture into three small bowls. Blend a drop of the red food coloring and strawberry extract into one bowl. Blend a drop of the green food coloring and mint extract into the second bowl. Add the vanilla extract to the third. Blend each mixture until creamy and smooth. Taste a little and add more flavoring if you want a stronger flavor.

3 Sprinkle the cutting board with confectioners' sugar. Place one of the balls of dough on the surface. Knead the dough until it is smooth and satiny. Return to bowl and cover with plastic wrap to keep it from drying out. Repeat this step with the other two balls of dough.

4 Line the baking sheets with parchment paper.

5 Lightly dust the cutting board with more confectioners' sugar. Use your fingers to roll one of the balls of dough into a 0.5-inch (1-cm) rope. Cut the rope into 0.5-inch (1-cm) pieces. Gently transfer the candies to a baking sheet. Repeat this step with the remaining two balls of dough.

6 Let the candies air dry at room temperature until firm, 1 to 2 days.

7 Store the candies in an airtight container with sheets of parchment paper between each layer. They will keep at room temperature for up to 2 weeks, or in the refrigerator for up to 1 month.

Kitchen Science
CANDY AND YOUR TEETH

You know that sugar is bad for your teeth. But do you know why? Bacteria live inside of your mouth. Most of them are harmless, even helpful. Some of them feed on food left on your teeth. As they eat, the bacteria produce an acid. The acid combines with your saliva to form plaque. The plaque wears holes in the tooth's surface, leading to cavities. Some foods wash away easily, but sticky candy stays on the teeth. This means candy is more likely to lead to cavities. Try only eating one or two pieces of candy at a time. Then brush your teeth. That's a good way to help prevent cavities.

Honeycomb Candy

What's all the buzz about? Honeycomb candy is as tasty as it is fun!
The baking soda makes bubbles that are trapped inside this candy. It
leaves a design that looks like a bee's honeycomb. Real honeycombs
are actually a collection of hexagon-shaped cells. Bees make them with
wax. They use them as nests and to store honey. You'll dip this candy
honeycomb in chocolate for an even sweeter taste.

INGREDIENTS	SUPPLIES
3/4 cup sugar	baking sheet
2 tablespoons honey	parchment paper
2 tablespoons water	nonstick cooking spray
1 1/2 teaspoons baking soda	medium saucepan
1/2 cup chocolate candy coating	measuring cups and spoons
	candy thermometer
	whisk or wooden spoon

1 Line the baking sheet with parchment paper. Spray with nonstick cooking spray.

2 In a medium saucepan, combine the sugar, honey, and water. Stir only enough to moisten the sugar. Attach a candy thermometer to the saucepan.

3 Cook over medium-high heat, without stirring. As the sugar melts, small bubbles will form, then larger bubbles. The sugar will begin to caramelize, turning golden brown. Heat to 300°F (adjusted for altitude if necessary), about 5 to 10 minutes. Do not stir. Remove the pan from the heat.

4 Quickly whisk the baking soda into the hot syrup. The syrup will foam up. Stir only enough to mix the ingredients, about 5 seconds.

5 Immediately pour the mixture onto the baking sheet. Don't spread out the candy, or the bubbles will pop. Allow the candy to cool until firm, about 1 hour. Break the candy into pieces.

6 Melt the candy coating according to package directions. Dip half of each piece of honeycomb candy into the chocolate coating. Let cool. Store candy in an airtight container in a dry, cool place.

TIP...

Sugar is hygroscopic. That means it attracts water. Honeycomb candy is mainly sugar. It will absorb moisture from the air. This can turn hard candy soft. If you live in a humid place, it is best to eat the candy within a day or two. In a dry climate, it may last up to two weeks if properly stored.

Kitchen Science

BUBBLY BAKING SODA ★

Baking soda is a type of salt. When heated above 175°F (79°C), baking soda creates a gas. This gas is carbon dioxide. The gas makes bubbles that help baked goods, such as cupcakes, rise. The same thing happens when the candy mixture is heated. The carbon dioxide creates bubbles. It's important not to mix the candy too much after adding the baking soda. This allows the air bubbles to stay large, creating the crispy honeycomb candy.

Peppermint Pull Taffy

Prepare to get some exercise with this recipe! Taffy's chewiness comes from one important step—pulling it. To "pull" taffy, stretch it out and then fold it back together, again and again. This aerates the taffy. Tiny air bubbles spread throughout the candy, making it lighter and chewier. Notice how the air bubbles in this candy cause a different texture than the air bubbles in the honeycomb candy. That's because of the different ingredients and techniques in making the candies.

INGREDIENTS

1 cup light corn syrup
3/4 cup sugar
2 tablespoons unsalted butter,
    plus extra for pulling the taffy
1 1/2 teaspoons peppermint
    extract
1/4 teaspoon salt
3 drops red food coloring

SUPPLIES

2 baking sheets
nonstick cooking spray
heavy small saucepan
measuring cups and spoons
candy thermometer
thick latex or latex-free gloves
pizza cutter
waxed paper

1 Spray the baking sheets with nonstick cooking spray. Set aside.

2 In the saucepan, combine the corn syrup and sugar. Attach a candy thermometer to the saucepan. Bring to a boil over medium heat. Add the butter and stir until melted. Continue heating and stirring until the temperature reaches 250°F (adjusted for altitude if necessary). Remove the saucepan from the heat.

3 Stir in the extract and salt. Pour half the mixture onto one baking sheet.

4 Add the food coloring to the remaining mixture and stir to combine. Pour the pink taffy onto the second baking sheet.

5 Let the taffy stand until it is cool enough to handle, about 5 to 10 minutes. Be careful—it may feel cool on the outside but still be very hot inside.

6 Put on thick latex or latex-free gloves. Then coat them well with butter. This keeps the taffy from sticking to the gloves. Pull and stretch the white taffy into a rope about 1 foot (30.5 cm) long. Fold the ends to meet and twist the two strands together. Repeat until the taffy loses its shine and becomes stiff. Pull the taffy into 0.5-inch- (1-cm-) thick ropes.

7 Repeat step 6 with the pink taffy. Try to get the same number of ropes of each color.

8 Take a rope of white taffy and a rope of pink taffy. Twist them together. Repeat until all the taffy has been twisted into white and pink ropes.

9 Use a pizza cutter to cut the taffy ropes into 1-inch (2-cm) pieces. Wrap each piece in waxed paper.

TIP......................................

When the taffy first comes out of the pan, it will be too hot to handle. Wait a few minutes so you don't burn your hands. But don't wait too long, or the taffy will harden.

Candy-Making Help

Not sure about something you're supposed to do in one of the recipes?
Look here for more information.

BOILING

All boiling is not the same. Understanding the different
stages of boiling will help you follow these recipes.

boiling—when bubbles rise and break on
the surface of the liquid

low boil or slow boil—a small number of
bubbles rise and break slowly

simmer—tiny bubbles break the surface
once in a while

boil rapidly or full rolling boil—many
bubbles cover the surface of the liquid

WHIPPING

To whip something, such as cream or eggs, beat it with
a whisk or mixer. This adds air to the ingredient.

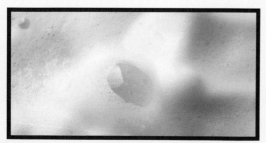

You can beat something until it becomes
foamy, or frothy (having tiny air bubbles).
Whipping also causes the ingredient
to thicken.

Some recipes may ask you to make stiff
peaks. Lift the beaters and you will see
peaks on the surface of the eggs or cream.
Stiff peaks should stand straight up.

Glossary

aerate—to introduce air into a material

bind—to combine with and hold together

caramelization—the process of cooking sugar until it turns brown

dissolve—to mix with a liquid and become part of the liquid

emulsion—a mixture of two or more liquids that resist combining

energy—the ability to do work; energy exists in several forms, including heat

evaporate—to turn from a liquid into a gas

heat—a kind of energy that makes things hot or warm

hygroscopic—easily absorbing moisture from the air

mixture—two or more substances that are mixed together but not binded

molecule—the smallest particle of a substance with the properties of that substance

reaction—a chemical change

saturated—holding as much water as possible

solution—the result of a solid, liquid, or gas being mixed with a liquid

supersaturated—concentrated beyond the saturation point

syrup—a thick, sweet liquid made by dissolving sugar in water

temperature—the measurement of heat or cold

Read More

Bolte, Mari. *In Good Taste: Great Gifts to Make, Eat, and Share.* Make It, Gift It. North Mankato, Minn.: Capstone Press, 2016.

Cobb, Vicki. *Science Experiments You Can Eat.* New York: HarperCollins, 2016.

Wheeler-Toppen, Jodi, and Carol Tennant. *Edible Science: Experiments You Can Eat.* Science and Nature. Washington, D.C.: National Geographic Society, 2015.

Internet Sites

Use FactHound to find Internet sites related to this book.

Visit *www.facthound.com*

Just type in 9781543510713 and go.

Check out projects, games and lots more at
www.capstonekids.com